"Come Zarafa" Atir whispered. "We must go now to Paris. Rise up."

Atir always spoke softly to the Giraffe. But today was a special day so there was a soft command in his voice. Today they would begin the walk to Paris. Who knew how far it was from Marseilles to Paris? But, his Honor, Saint-Hilare was certain to know. He seemed a gentle man, and he loved La Giraffe. So it would be well.

"There she is," thought Saint-Hilaire, "what a graceful and elegant animal." She warmed his heart immediately. La Giraffe welcomed him with her large eyes and knew <u>he</u> was the one to walk to Paris with her.

Always beside La Giraffe was Atir and Hassan, who had come from Egypt in Africa to care for her.

The morning of the second day brought a chance to show La Giraffe to the people of Cours Miraeau in Aix-en-Provence.

In front of the procession are three cows to provide La Giraffe with 26 litres of milk each day. She loved the cows and would follow them anywhere.

What the children had were questions. The most puzzling was "Can you say what is a Giraffe?" Saint-Hilaire constructed a visual picture of the name for a Giraffe: a combination of a camel and a leopard, therefore the "official scientific name" is cameleopardis.

A final question from a nine year old boy was answered by Atir. "Can I sleep with La Giraffe tonight." "Certainly, mon enfant" in Atir's broken French. The boy touched the soft fur of Zarafa and smiled, looking forward to his treat beside this incredible animal.

That night in the stable Hassan gave
Marcel a lesson on the geography of the Mediterranean Sea.

"There is a large sea that flows from Marseilles to Egypt in Africa." said Hassan.
"There is a city called Alexandria where ships take goods and Zarafa everywhere."

"Do other animals live there with Zarafa?" asked Marcel.The men nodded, "Yes,
many animals in Africa …"

One might ask, "Why is the Giraffe going to Paris? For what reason?" In the time of this story – and the Giraffe's story is true – a way for one country to show friendship to another country was to give a marvelous gift to the ruler of that country.

In 1827, the Viceroy of Egypt wished for the friendship of the King of France. Therefore, the Viceroy sent men to central Africa to find a young Giraffe to take to the King as an amazing gift.

This gift would be special because there had never been a Giraffe in France – everyone would be seeing their *first* giraffe!

It was north of Orgon that a girl of 14 asked if she could ride on La Giraffe. Her mother was there and explained that Entienne was an expert rider, therefore no danger. Saint-Hilaire smiled and nodded, so the girl was allowed a short ride holding a velvet rope around the neck of La Giraffe.

Every night, in all the towns, Saint-Hilaire was asked to show his prize to the local people. In Valence, it was the home of an officer at the Artillery School. The crowd was pleased with the gentle Giraffe, but also to have as a guest the famous scientist Geoffroy Saint-Hilaire, one of those to accompany Napoleon to Egypt in 1798.

"Your Honor," a woman asked Saint-Hilaire, "what can La Giraffe think of our lovely France?" Saint-Hilaire said he would indeed be the greatest of scientists if he could know the senses and feelings of animals. "Consider, Mademoiselle, this unique beast comes from a land and nature so pure and thoughtless that the intellect we seek is not useful. What is useful is La Giraffe's ability to see further than any animal.

A man yells at Atir, "I don't want my dog to bite La Giraffe. He might hurt her."

Atir bows toward the man. "Not to be worried, good Sir. Zarafa will not be harmed by your dog … alas, we need to move your dog away. Zarafa can kick a lion to death in a moment."

Man, "Non?"

Atir, "Yes, yes, mon amie."

Your Honor," said the old woman, " your giraffe looks well beside our monument and is almost as large. How tall is she?"

"Now she is 12 feet. Six inches taller than when she arrived in Marseille six months ago." He smiled at her, "some giraffes reach a height of 16 feet."

Lyon

Valence

Orange

Orgon

Avignon

Aix-en-Provence

Marseille

Prove

As the entourage found itself 17 days away from Marseilles, Saint-Hilaire saw La Giraffe was in good health, but she was getting tired. At Lyon, Saint-Hilaire saw that it would be possible to board a Riverboat and move several days closer to Paris with less effort.

At the boat dock it seemed that all of Lyon had come to see La Giraffe off on her River trip toward Paris.

It was here that Saint-Hilaire realized this journey had its most important value of showing La Giraffe to the people of France. Imagine, their "first Giraffe."

Alpes

Sailing toward Paris, all were pleased to have four days rest and watch France pass by them.

Saint-Hilaire spoke to the Captain of the Boat. "So, now we sail on the River Saône. La Giraffe is no stranger to rivers, she has navigated the Nile." The Captain looked puzzled.

Saint-Hilaire continued, "The Nile River in Egypt, where La Giraffe came from."

"Non, this Giraffe?" said the Captain as if he were hearing a fairy story.

Atir had grown to love Zarafa as if they were brother and sister. As they flowed down this River it seemed to Atir that he always wished to say to Zarafa, "What are your thoughts, beautiful one?"

"Olà there, can you say something to me?"

They looked up to see a man with wild hair. "Can you tell me why your animal has such short horns covered with hair … and how long is that tongue?"

Atir looked up to the man and said, "The horns are called ossicones. They are like bone and covered with skin."

Saint-Hilaire said, "Sir, the tongue of La Giraffe, it is 20 inches long, just right for licking leaves off of Linden trees."

The man smiled down at them and waved. "Bon chance, La Giraffe. Good journey to Paris … bless the King for me."

Many children and their parents
along the journey asked most simple questions …

"How does a Giraffe sleep?"

Or, "… where does her head lie?" Or, "How does this animal work???"

Hassan and Atir had been asked these questions before, so they had practiced
in the evenings as Zarafa was preparing for sleep.

Then, just outside Paris, a child raised this question and they were prepared.
In the meadow, Hassan said to La Giraffe, "Sleep now, Zarafa. Show these
lovely children how you sleep … " Atir kneeled alongside Zarafa and
encouraged her with whispers.

… and so for them, Zarafa lay down and pretended to sleep.

Only they, and his Honor knew that La Giraffe needed little sleep …

Paris! The end of a journey that was 4,000 miles from Central
Africa to Alexandria, across the Mediterranean Sea to Marseille. Then
the last 532 kilometers, walking to Paris –16 kilometers each day.

La Giraffe was greeted in Paris by 50,000 of its citizens, each eager to see their first ever Giraffe. She was a beauty that day, looking far ahead for the King of France.

Saint-Hilaire had arranged for one of France's leading artists to be present on this historic day to record with paint and brush this amazing moment of the first giraffe to walk through Paris.

"Your Highness, I have the pleasure of presenting a gift from His Excellency, The Viceroy Mohammed Ali of Egypt. His gift wishes friendship and cooperation between our two countries."

Saint-Hilaire paused and looked at La Giraffe, his King and the people of Paris. This would be a special moment in <u>his</u> life.

"I also bring greetings from your subjects from Marseille to Paris. All of whom had the good fortune of a pleasant meeting with La Giraffe. Be assured that they love her. Indeed, all of France love their first giraffe.

We are fortunate this gentle creature has blessed us with her presence."

Atir volunteered to stay and live with Zarafa in her special place, to care for her, and tell visitors about her journey from central Africa to the Paris Zoo.

Now, each night after the last of the day's visitors had gone, La Giraffe and Atir settled down for a peaceful night's rest with a special sleeping shelf for Atir. The last words heard each night were,

"Good night, Zarafa."   "Good night, Atir"   "Sleep well …"

The Giraffe who walked to Paris

For JESSICA

Written by Dirk Wales

Illustrated by
Bridgette Comellas

GREAT PLAINS PRESS

1103 Canyon Road, Suite B • Santa Fe, New Mexico 87501

© copyright 2014